Amarillo

Dallas

Ft. Worth

El Paso

Austin   Houston

San Antonio

Gulf Coast

T is for Texas

written by kids
for kids

WESTWINDS
PRESS®

A is for **Armadillo**

Our state animal has a very strong shell.
It's tougher than nails, just like Texas, as well.

B is for **Bluebonnet**

The Texas bluebonnet is the most beautiful by far.

Its tall blue flowers really make it a star.

C

is for

Capital

Austin is the capital of
our great state;
The place where our
congressmen legislate.

D

is for **Dallas**

Known as Big D for its huge population—

As a matter of fact, it's ranked ninth in the nation.

E is for Enchanted Rock

One of our state's awesome natural parks.

Come visit and see the cool, pink granite rock.

F

is for **Football**

Friday Night Lights is a Texas tradition!
And for many kids here it's a major ambition.

G is for Gulf Coast

The Gulf Coast is where we go to have fun.

We fish and swim and build sand castles in the sun.

H is for **Horned Lizard**

The Texas horned lizard is an unusual creature—
Squirting blood from its eyes is its strangest feature.

I is for

Independent

We were once the most independent state, by far,

Which is why we are known for our flag's Lone Star.

J

is for **Juneteenth**

Juneteenth was a great day for our state. Yes, indeed!
June 19 was the day Texas slaves were finally freed.

K is for **K-9**

These police dogs help to fight crime.

They're catching criminals one at a time!

Jax (shown above) works with Deputy McCorkle for the Ellis County, Texas, Sheriff's Office.

L is for **Longhorns**

Longhorns are tough, longhorns are strong.

Check out those cows! Texas longhorns have brawn.

M

is for
Mariachi Music

A trumpet, violins, and a couple guitars
Make this music a shining Texas star!

N

is for **nASA**

Mission control calls Johnson Space Center home.

They give the directions so astronauts know where to roam.

O

is for **Oil**

Oil fields have been here since the days of old.
If you are from Texas, then you call it black gold.

P is for

Prickly Pear Cactus

This flowering cactus has thorns that will poke.

If one sticks you, it will not be a joke.

Q

is for

Quinceañera

A Hispanic girl's
coming of age—
We celebrate the
turning of a new page.

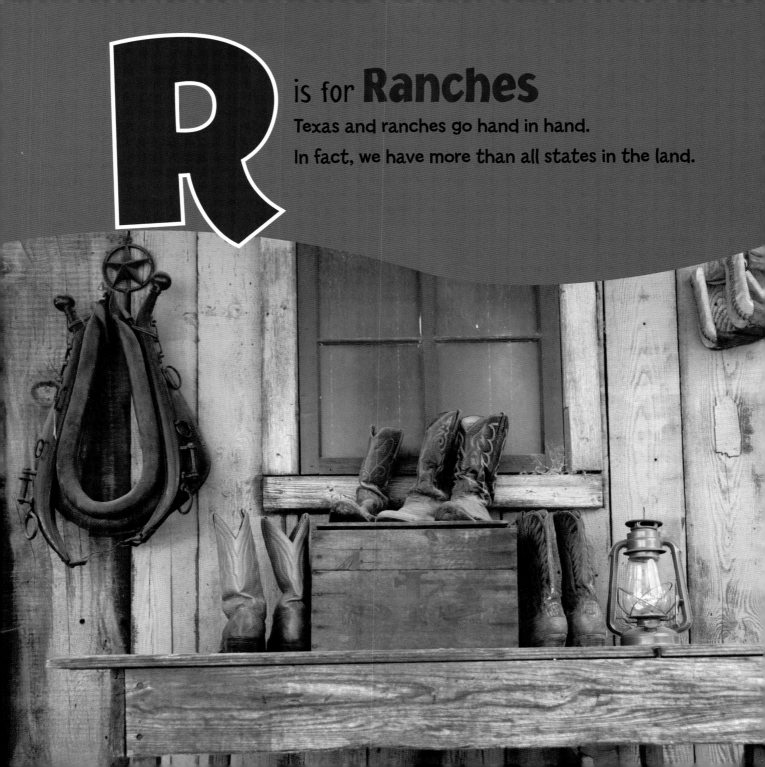

R is for Ranches

Texas and ranches go hand in hand.

In fact, we have more than all states in the land.

S is for

State Fair

The Texas Star Ferris wheel is one really tall ride;

And from bacon to Twinkies, you can bet the food's fried.

T is for **Tribes**

Native American tribes helped write our state's past;

Kickapoo, Alabama-Coushatta, and Tigua* Pueblo—their legacies last.

*pronounced Tiwa

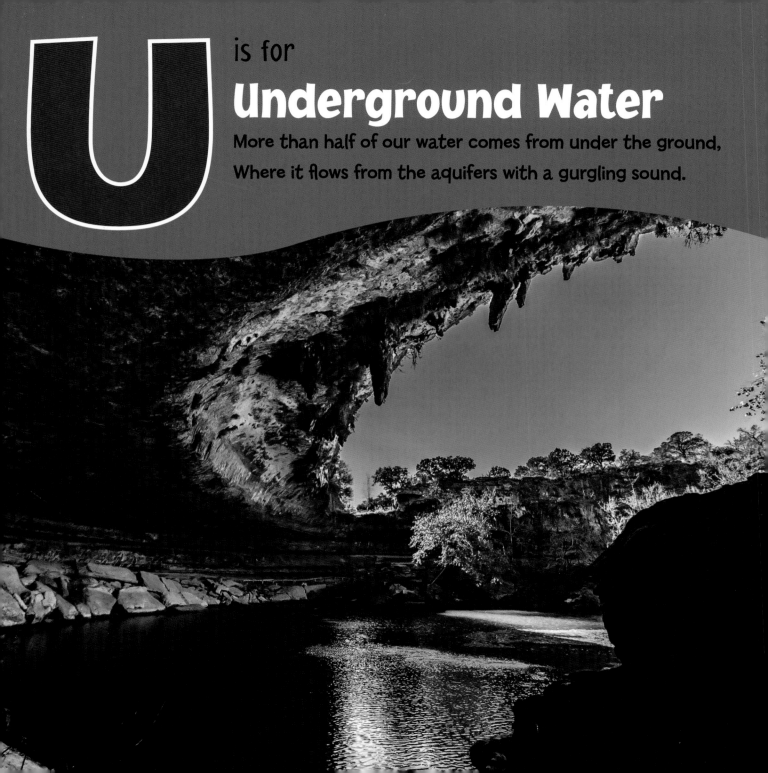

U is for

Underground Water

More than half of our water comes from under the ground,
Where it flows from the aquifers with a gurgling sound.

V is for Vaqueros

Vaqueros, the first cowboys, stood tall in the saddle.

Across the Texas range they rode, rounding up cattle.

W is for **Western Swing**

Western swing is the dance that will make your boots scoot
At the dance halls in Texas—you're sure to have a hoot!

X is for X Marks the Spot

Jean Lafitte and his pirates loved to pillage and plunder,
And X marks the spot that their treasure is under.

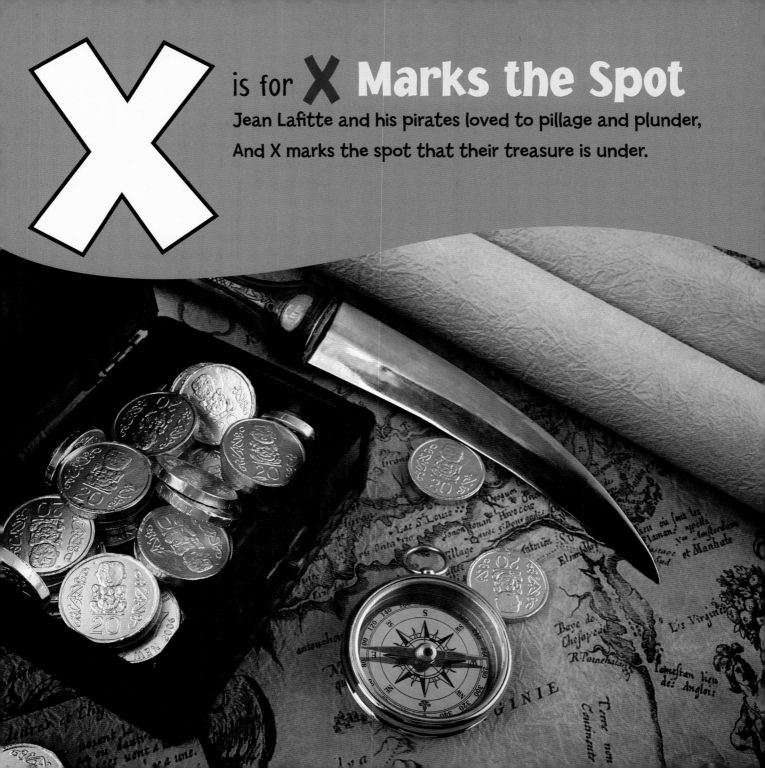

is for **Yummy**

Pecan pie is the official
dessert of our state.
Just cut a big slice and
put it right on my plate.

Z is for **Zoo**

The San Antonio Zoo has more than nine thousand creatures.
Cute baby tigers are just one of its features.

Who Knew?

Armadillo

Armadillo means "little armored one" in Spanish, so called because this tough guy is covered in hard, flexible scales. The nine-banded armadillo is the state mammal of Texas. When frightened, an armadillo can jump up to four feet in the air, making it a real hazard on Texas roads and earning it the nickname "Hillbilly Speed Bump."

Bluebonnet

The bluebonnet was named for its brilliant color and unique shape, which looks like a lady's hat. Texans really love bluebonnets! They adopted it as their state flower in 1901 and host the annual Bluebonnet Festival in Burnet, the "Bluebonnet Capital of Texas."

Capital

Did you know the State Capitol Building in Austin is the largest in the US—seven feet higher than the one in Washington DC! The capital city's motto is "Keep Austin Weird." And what's really weird is that it's got the largest urban bat population in the world! 1.5 million Mexican free-tailed bats live under the Congress Avenue Bridge. Yikes!

Dallas

They say, "Everything is bigger in Texas!" And Dallas, the ninth *biggest* city in the US, is home to some really *BIG* attractions. Fifty-five-foot-tall "Big Tex" is the *biggest* cowboy in the world, greeting visitors to Dallas's State Fair of Texas. The Dallas Cowboys play in a stadium so *big* that the Statue of Liberty could stand up inside it. Dallas is also home to the *biggest* indoor Christmas tree—ninety-five feet tall and topped with a hundred-pound star!

Enchanted Rock

This pink granite dome, the largest of its kind in the country, was formed when the softer earth around it eroded, leaving the harder granite exposed. Humans have been telling spooky stories about this rock for thousands of years: ghost fires flicker on it at night, it's a portal to other worlds, and if you sleep on it you'll wake up invisible! Enchanted, indeed!

Football

Did you know the Dallas Cowboys are the only NFL team to have twenty straight winning seasons? Pretty impressive! But the Cowboys aren't Texans' only football favorites. In Austin, they root for the University of Texas Longhorns. If you listen closely, you might hear fans shouting their motto: "Hook 'em Horns!"

Gulf Coast

The Gulf Coast stretches along the Gulf of Mexico, providing Texas with 600 miles of beaches. The marshes, bays, and estuaries are not only beautiful, but are great habitat for coastal animals, including muskrats, bottlenose dolphins, alligators, and tons of birds.

Horned Lizard

Bet you didn't know lizards could have superpowers. Well, the Texas horned lizard does! When threatened, it can inflate its body, doubling in size like a prickly balloon! And if something is still dumb enough to attack it, this lizard will squirt it with a stream of *blood* up to five feet from the corners of its eyes. Yuck!

Independent

Believe it or not, Texas was its own country for *ten years* before it became part of the US! Texas Independence Day celebrates the signing of the Declaration of Independence on March 2, 1836. That's when Texans broke away from Mexico and founded the Republic of Texas. Texas didn't become a part of the United States until December 1845. The lone white star on the Texas flag represents that independent spirit.

Facts about the

Juneteenth

On June 19 (Get it? June-teenth!) 1865, Union soldiers freed slaves throughout the state. Today, Texans celebrate with parades, barbecues, and strawberry soda (the traditional Juneteenth drink). Juneteenth is so popular it even has its own flag!

K-9

All over Texas, police dogs (called K-9s) are trained to help with law enforcement. Most K-9s are considered full-fledged police officers: they get a badge and everything! K-9s even wear bullet-proof vests when they're sent into dangerous situations. Different breeds have different talents: Bloodhounds do search and rescue, while beagles sniff out drugs and explosives. But the trusty German shepherd is the most common breed taking a bite out of crime!

Longhorns

Texas longhorns really live up to their name: their horns can span five, six, or even seven feet. In 2012, a bull named Johnny Reb earned the Guinness World Record for his massive horns, which measured nine feet, three inches from tip to tip! While a bull may hold the record, in general, female longhorns have the biggest horns.

Mariachi Music

This folk music comes from Mexico and combines the sounds of violins, trumpets, and guitars. Musicians wear traditional *charro* suits, which were originally worn by Mexican cowboys, and consist of wide-brimmed hats called *sombreros* and black suits with intricate silver embroidery.

NASA

Is the moon made of cheese? The folks at Houston's Lyndon B. Johnson Space Center can tell you. It's home to the lunar samples astronauts brought back from their first trip to the moon. These space rocks are stored in a special vault and kept in a pure nitrogen environment, which mimics the atmosphere of the moon and protects the rocks.

Oil

In 1901, when the Lucas No. 1 well blew at the Spindletop oil field in Beaumont, it was the largest oil strike the world had ever seen! Texas is still the leading crude-oil producer, pumping out nearly three million barrels a day (that's over one-third of all oil produced in the US). Texas is also the leading producer of natural gas and wind-powered energy.

Prickly Pear Cactus

The spines on Texas's state cactus are not to be messed with—they can grow up to three inches long! In summer, the pads grow an edible fruit (called a "tuna"), which Native Americans have been eating for thousands of years. In addition to food, the prickly pear provides shelter for some: the desert pack rat makes its den inside the base of the cactus.

Quinceañera

This Spanish word meaning "fifteenth birthday" is also what Texans call the huge party thrown on this day. It's a coming-of-age tradition that can be traced back to 500 BC, when Aztec girls were given the instructions and responsibilities of womanhood. Today, it's traditional for the birthday girl to wear a ball gown, a tiara, and a pair of fancy high heels, all to show her new adult status.

great state of Texas!

Ranches

Texas has more ranchland than any other state, covering over 130 million acres! The King Ranch, one of the world's largest ranches, is bigger than the state of Rhode Island! Founded in 1853, it was Texas's first ranch, and today more than 60,000 cattle and 300 quarter horses call it home.

State Fair

Each year, three million visitors come to Dallas to check out the fair's attractions, including the Texas Star, its 212-foot Ferris wheel! But the fair may be best known for its crazy deep-fried menu. Of course there are corn dogs, but have you ever tried deep-fried Oreos, Twinkies, or s'mores? They even have deep-fried banana splits! YUM!

Tribes

Everywhere you turn in Texas, Native American history is all around you. Many towns—like Waxahachie, Anahuac, and Nacogdoches—are named for Native words. Even the word *Texas* has Native roots. It comes from *teysha*, which means "friend" in the language of the Caddo Indians. When Spanish settlers arrived, they used *teysha* to name the land around them and to greet their neighbors: "Howdy, friend!"

Underground Water

Texas gets over half of its water from underground reservoirs called aquifers. Texans tap into them for drinking water, industry, and irrigation. The good news: large areas that don't get enough rain have big aquifers beneath them. The bad news: some aquifers are being drained faster than rain can fill them back up. Many Texans are working on ways to conserve this precious state resource.

Vaqueros

If it weren't for the vaqueros of Mexico, we might not have the American cowboys we know and love today. Long before Texas was a state, Spanish settlers in Mexico began herding the millions of longhorn cattle that roamed free there. Later, they moved north into the land we now call Texas, and continued their cattle-driving tradition. Much of what Texas cowboys know, they learned from their vaquero friends.

Western Swing

Western swing, the official state music of Texas, is a popular dance style that was invented in Texas in the 1930s. Western swing is typically played by a string band, along with steel guitar and drums, among other instruments. Before it got the name Western swing, some called it "novelty hot dance," "cowboy jazz," and even "hillbilly music."

X Marks the Spot

For years, infamous French pirate Jean Lafitte plundered Spanish ships in the Gulf of Mexico. Then, in 1817, he grew bolder, taking over the town of Galveston, Texas, and making Galveston Island his pirating base. But when his crew attacked US ships, Lafitte knew his luck had run out. To avoid capture, he burned Galveston to the ground, took his favorite ship and best men, and sailed off into the sunset! Some folks say before he left, Lafitte buried his treasure on Galveston Island. To this day, no one has found it. Will you be the lucky one?

Yummy

Texans are nutty for pecans! It's the state tree, the state nut, *and* the state dessert (pecan pie, that is). *Pecan* is an Algonquian word meaning "a nut requiring a stone to crack," and was a popular food for Native Americans long before Europeans arrived in Texas. Turns out pecans are an ideal food source, since they provide way more calories than most meat.

Zoo

In 2014, the San Antonio Zoo celebrated its 100th birthday! When it opened in 1914, it had only elk, buffalo, deer, monkeys, two lions, and four bears. Today, it covers fifty-six acres and is home to more than 9,000 animals. The zoo is known for its breeding programs for endangered species (they've successfully bred fifty-three endangered snow leopards since 1970!), but its most unusual resident is probably Thelma and Louise, the two-headed turtle born in 2013.

Thank you to everyone at Boys & Girls Clubs of Greater Fort Worth for encouraging your kids to write and enter this contest. Thank you to the dedicated staff, Matt Sinclair, Juanita Holguin, Jessica Soto, and the team at the Clubs' North Fort Worth branch, who guided the youth through this process. And thanks to Robyn Best . . . for everything! But most of all, thanks to the kids who wrote such fantastic poetry for this book. **Way to go**!

Boys & Girls Clubs of Greater Fort Worth focuses on providing disadvantaged youth with enriching programs that lead to academic success, healthy lifestyles, and positive character and citizenship. Club youth benefit from a safe, positive environment, supportive relationships with caring adults and mentors, unique educational and career opportunities, and a variety of fun programs that help build an optimistic foundation for the future. To learn more about the Boys & Girls Clubs of Greater Fort Worth, visit our website at **www.fortworthkids.org**.

Photo of youth from Boys & Girls Clubs of Greater Fort Worth / Back Row (left to right) Nicholas Aguilar, Quashanna Williams, Ricardo Aguilar, Anthony Ayala, Andrew Alvarado, Norma Martinez, Erika Martinez **Middle Row** Sebastian Lopez, Ernest Manzo, Brianna Burgos, Andrew Ponce, Marcus Miles, Jacob Hernandez **Front Row** Monserrath Gomez, Keilani Gonzalez, John Gomez, Kurt Ireta, Jacob Ibarra

Nicholas Aguilar (M)

Ricardo Aguilar (X)

Adrian Alvarado (O)

Andrew Alvarado (L, N, R, Y, Z)

Anthony Ayala (T)

Brianna Burgos (G, J, V)

Rey'ana Cerda (D, I)

John Gomez (K)

Monserrath Gomez (A, B)

Daisy Gonzalez (C, E)

Keilani Gonzalez (U)

Jacob Hernandez

Jacob Ibarra

Kurt Ireta (N, P, Z)

Vianney Ireta (Q)

Sebastian Lopez (H)

Stephanie Lopez (W)

Erika Martinez (S)

Norma Martinez

Ernest Manzo

Marcus Miles (F)

Andrew Ponce

Quashanna Williams

The following photographers hold copyright to their images as indicated: iStock.com/irin717, **A**; iStock.com/Dean Fikar, **B**; iStock.com/egearing, **C**; iStock.com/Aneese, **D, O**; Richard McMillin/Dreamstime.com, **E**; Joe Gallo, **F, K**; Rob Tilley/DanitaDelimont.com, **G**; iStock.com/Marilyn Haddrill, **H**; iStock.com/Lanier, **I**; Calyx22/Dreamstime.com, **J**; iStock.com/DHuss, **L**; iStock.com/DOUGBERRY, **M**; Michael DeFreitas/DanitaDelimont.com, **N**; iStock.com/Lokibaho, **P**; iStock.com/GemaBlanton, **Q**; iStock.com/EyeJoy, **R**; Anthony Aneese Totah Jr./Dreamstime.com, **S**; Bill Pogue/Mira.com, **T**; Richard McMillin/Dreamstime.com, **U**; iStock.com/GomezDavid, **V**; iStock.com/Jason York, **W**; iStock.com/Fyletto, **X**; Monkey Business Images/Dreamstime.com, **Y**; San Antonio Zoo, **Z**.

Library of Congress Cataloging-in-Publication Data
T is for Texas : written by kids for kids / Michelle McCann.
     pages cm. — (See my state)
  ISBN 978-0-88240-989-4 (hardback)
 1. Texas—Juvenile literature. 2. Texas—History—Juvenile literature. I. McCann, Michelle Roehm, 1968- editor of compilation.
  F386.3.T25 2014
  976.4—dc23
                                     2014013393

Editor: Michelle McCann
Designer: Vicki Knapton

Published by WestWinds Press®
An imprint of

GRAPHIC ARTS
BOOKS®

P.O. Box 56118
Portland, Oregon 97238-6118
503-254-5591
www.graphicartsbooks.com

Printed in China